Easy Crochet Sweaters & Shawls

The Ultimate Guide To Crochet Sweaters & Shawls

Copyright © 2023

All rights reserved.

DEDICATION

The author and publisher have provided this e-book to you for your personal use only. You may not make this e-book publicly available in any way. Copyright infringement is against the law. If you believe the copy of this e-book you are reading infringes on the author's copyright, please notify the publisher at: https://us.macmillan.com/piracy

Contents

Simple Crochet Jacket 1

Girls Sweater 14

Tapestry Crochet Fisherman's Sweater 26

Lace Crochet Shawl 43

Summer Nights Crochet Shawl 51

Easy Crochet Sweaters & Shawls

Simple Crochet Jacket

Supplies:

- Lion Brand Twisted Cotton Blend: (Weight: 5/Bulky yarn weight - 98 yds, 3.5 oz)

- Tan/Ecru (#765-209) – 10 (11, 13, 15, 16, 17, 18) skeins [(approx.

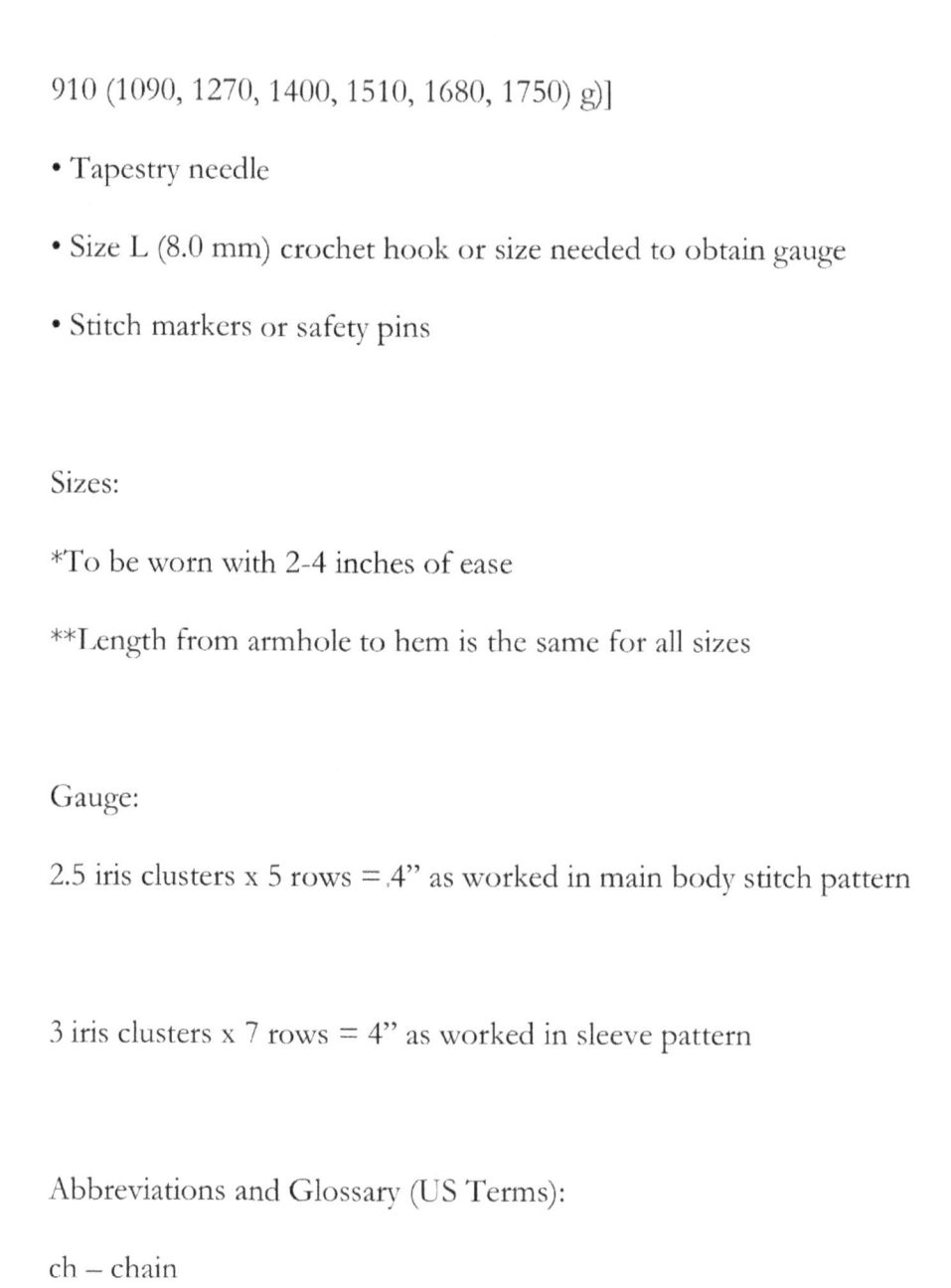

Easy Crochet Sweaters & Shawls

910 (1090, 1270, 1400, 1510, 1680, 1750) g)]

- Tapestry needle

- Size L (8.0 mm) crochet hook or size needed to obtain gauge

- Stitch markers or safety pins

Sizes:

*To be worn with 2-4 inches of ease

**Length from armhole to hem is the same for all sizes

Gauge:

2.5 iris clusters x 5 rows = 4" as worked in main body stitch pattern

3 iris clusters x 7 rows = 4" as worked in sleeve pattern

Abbreviations and Glossary (US Terms):

ch – chain

Easy Crochet Sweaters & Shawls

ch1sp – space created by 1 chain

dc – double crochet

hdc – half double crochet

PM – place marker

rep – repeat

RS – right side

sc – single crochet

sk – skip

slst – slip stitch

st(s) – stitch(es)

tch – turning chain

WS – wrong side

Overall Pattern Notes:

- Ch 3 counts as 1 dc throughout.

To check gauge:

Foundation Row: Ch 18.

Row 1: Sc in 2nd ch from hook and in each ch to end of row; turn. [17 sc]

Row 2: Ch 3, *sk 2 sc, (2 dc, ch 1, 2 dc) in the next sc; rep from * until 2 sc remain, sk 1 sc, 1 dc in last sc; turn. [5 Iris clusters, 2 dc]

Row 3: Ch 3, sk first 3 dc, *(2 dc, ch 1, 2 dc) in ch1sp, sk next 4 dc, rep from * until last ch1sp, (2 dc, ch 1, 2 dc) in ch1sp, sk 2 dc, 1 dc in tch, turn.

Rep Row 3 five more times for 8 rows in total. Measure in center 4" square of swatch and compare to gauge listed above. If square includes more stitches than the listed gauge, increase hook size and try again. If square includes fewer stitches than the listed gauge, decrease hook size and try again.

Easy Crochet Sweaters & Shawls

Notes:

- Fronts and Back are worked in one piece until dividing for the armholes.

Foundation Row: Ch 66 (78, 93, 99, 108, 117, 126).

Row 1 (RS): Sc in 2nd ch from hook and in each ch to end of row; turn. [65 (77, 92, 98, 107, 116, 125) sc]

Row 2 (WS): Ch 3, *sk 2 sc, (2 dc, ch 1, 2 dc) in the next sc; rep from * until 2 sc remain, sk 1 sc, 1 dc in last sc; turn. [21 (25, 30, 32, 35, 38, 41) Iris clusters, 2 dc]

Row 3 (RS): Ch 3, sk first 3 dc, *(2 dc, ch 1, 2 dc) in ch1sp, sk next 4 dc, rep from * until last ch1sp, (2 dc, ch 1, 2 dc) in ch1sp, sk 2 dc, 1 dc in tch; turn.

Repeat Row 3 nineteen more times. Piece should now contain a total of 21 cluster rows for all sizes (which does not include Row 1.) Do not fasten off. If you would like a longer sweater, simply add more rows in multiples of 2 to end with a WS row.

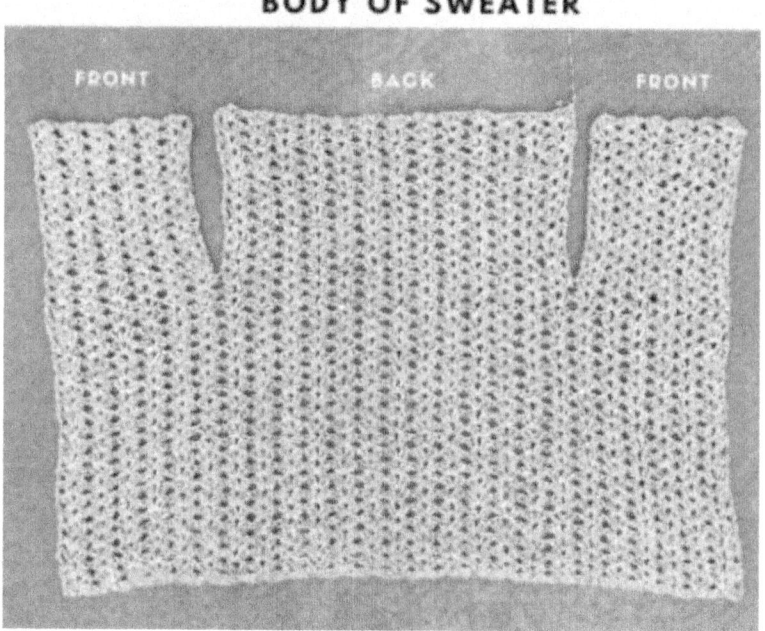

BODY OF SWEATER

NOTES:

Sweater is now worked in three separate columns: Left Front, Right Front and Back. Main Body stitch pattern continues.

Count 5 (6, 7, 7, 8, 9, 10) clusters in from both Right and Left sides, PM in ch1sp of 5th (6th, 7th, 7th, 8th, 9th, 10th) clusters. Markers indicate edge of armhole.

First Front:

With working yarn still attached:

Row 1 (RS): Ch 3, sk first 3 dc, (2 dc, ch 1, 2 dc) in first ch1sp, *sk next 4 dc, (2 dc, ch 1, 2 dc) in next ch1sp; rep from * 3 (4, 5, 5, 6, 7, 8) more times, sk 1 dc, 1 dc in last dc of marked cluster; turn. [5 (6, 7, 7, 8, 9, 10) Iris clusters, 2 dc]

Row 2 (WS): Ch 3, sk first 3 dc, (2 dc, ch 1, 2 dc) in first ch1sp, *sk next 4 dc, (2 dc, ch 1, 2 dc) in next ch1sp; rep from * to last 3 sts, sk 2 dc, 1 dc in top of tch; turn.

[Repeat Row 2] 9 (10, 11, 12, 12, 13, 13) more times for a total of 11 (12, 13, 14, 14, 15, 15) rows. Fasten off.

With RS facing, attach yarn in last dc of marked cluster to the right of marker on opposite (unworked) side of piece. (Left handed: left side of marker.)

Row 1 (RS): Ch 3, sk first 2 dc of marked cluster, (2 dc, ch 1 , 2 dc) in marked ch1sp, *sk next 4 dc, (2 dc, ch 1, 2 dc) in next ch1sp; rep from * to last 3 sts , sk 2 dc, 1 dc in top of tch; turn. [5 (6, 7, 7, 8, 9, 10) Iris clusters, 2 dc]

Row 2 (WS): Ch 3, sk first 2 dc, (2 dc, ch 1, 2 dc) in next ch1sp, *sk next 4 dc, (2 dc, ch 1, 2 dc) in next ch1sp; rep from * to end, sk 1 dc, 1 dc in top of tch; turn.

[Repeat Row 2] 9 (10, 11, 12, 12, 13, 13) more times for a total of 11 (12, 13, 14, 14, 15, 15) rows. Fasten off.

Back:

Notes:

- Back is worked over remaining 11 (13, 16, 18, 19, 20, 21) unworked clusters in between fronts.

With RS facing, attach yarn in the first dc of next unworked cluster between fronts.

Row 1 (RS): Ch 3, sk first 2 dc, (2 dc, ch 1, 2 dc) in first ch1sp, *sk next 4 dc, (2 dc, ch 1, 2 dc) in next ch1sp; rep from * to last 2 dc, sk next dc, 1 dc in last dc of cluster; turn. [11 (13, 16, 18, 19, 20, 21) Iris clusters, 2 dc]

Row 2 (WS): Ch 3, sk first 2 dc, (2 dc, ch 1, 2 dc) in next ch1sp, *sk next 4 dc, (2 dc, ch 1, 2 dc) in next ch1sp; rep from * to end, 1 dc in turning ch. [11 (13, 16, 18, 19, 20, 21) Iris clusters, 2 dc]

[Repeat Row 2] 9 (10, 11, 12, 12, 13, 13) more times for a total of 11 (12, 13, 14, 14, 15, 15) rows. Fasten off.

Fold RS of sweater Fronts to sweater Back. Pin in place taking care to line up stitches of Front and Back pieces. Use tapestry needle and mattress stitch to join Right Front to Back and Left Front to Back at shoulders.

Border

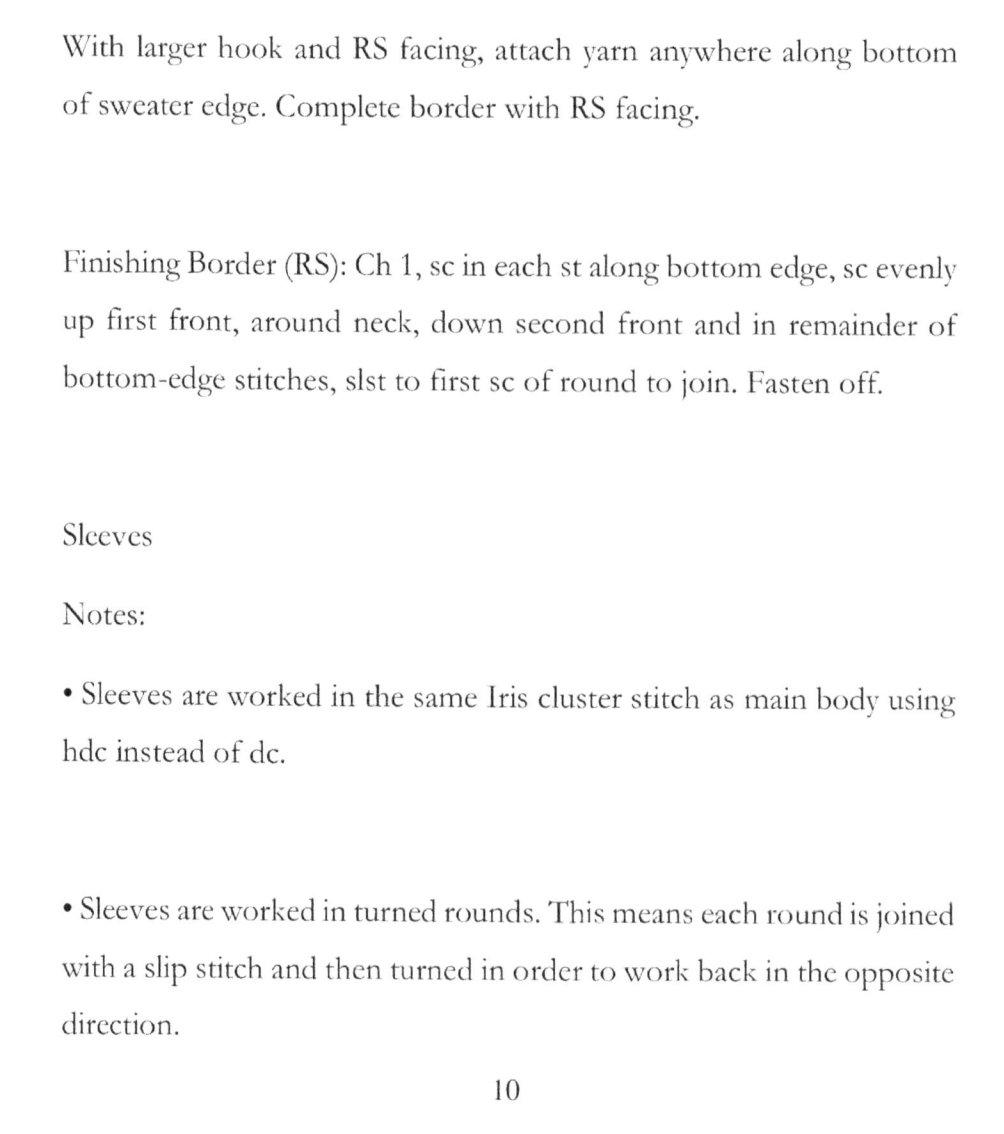

With larger hook and RS facing, attach yarn anywhere along bottom of sweater edge. Complete border with RS facing.

Finishing Border (RS): Ch 1, sc in each st along bottom edge, sc evenly up first front, around neck, down second front and in remainder of bottom-edge stitches, slst to first sc of round to join. Fasten off.

Sleeves

Notes:

• Sleeves are worked in the same Iris cluster stitch as main body using hdc instead of dc.

• Sleeves are worked in turned rounds. This means each round is joined with a slip stitch and then turned in order to work back in the opposite direction.

- Ch-2 at the beginning of each round counts as 1 hdc throughout.

Make 2.

With RS facing, attach yarn at bottom of armhole.

Round 1 (RS): Ch 1, place 43 (47, 51, 59, 63, 67, 67) sc evenly around armhole; sl st to first sc of round to join; turn. [43 (47, 51, 59, 63, 67, 67) sc]

Round 2 (WS): Ch 2, sk first 3 sc, (2 hdc, ch 1, 2 hdc) in next sc, *sk 3 sc, (2 hdc, ch 1, 2 hdc) in next sc; rep from * until 3 sts remain, sk 2 sc, 1 hdc in last sc, slst to top of tch to join; turn. [10 (11, 12, 14, 15, 16, 16) hdc Iris clusters, 2 hdc]

Note: To make sure the sleeve is centered properly: for sizes M and 3X, ensure the 6th (M) and 8th (3X) cluster is at the shoulder seam;

for sizes XS/S, L/1X, 1X/2X, 4X, and 5X ensure the shoulder seam is between the 5th & 6th, 6th & 7th, 7th & 8th, 8th & 9th, and 8th & 9th clusters for each size, respectively.

Round 3 (RS): Ch 2, sk tch, 1 hdc in next st, *sk 2 hdc, (2 hdc, ch 1, 2 hdc) in next ch1sp, sk 2 hdc; rep from * to end of round; sl st to top of tch to join; turn. [10 (11, 12, 14, 15, 16, 16) hdc Iris clusters, 2 hdc]

Round 4 (WS): Ch 2, sk tch, *sk 2 hdc, (2 hdc, ch 1, 2 hdc) in next ch1sp, sk 2 hdc; rep from * to last st, 1 hdc in last hdc, slst to top of tch to join; turn. [10 (11, 12, 14, 15, 16, 16) hdc Iris clusters, 2 hdc]

[Rep Rounds 3 & 4] 9 (10, 9, 8, 8, 8, 7) more times then [rep Round 3] 1 (0, 0, 1, 0, 1, 0) more time(s). Sleeve should now contain a total of 23 (24, 22, 21, 20, 21, 18) rounds and measure 14 (14.5, 13.25, 12.75, 12, 12.75, 11.5)". After last round, do not turn (turn, turn, do not turn, turn, do not turn, turn) to have RS facing.

If a longer sleeve length is desired, work additional repeats of Rounds

3 & 4 as desired, if ending on Round 3, do not turn to keep RS facing.

Finishing Border (RS): Ch 1, sc in top of tch, sc in next hdc, *sc in first hdc of next cluster, sc in next ch1sp, sc in last hdc of same cluster; rep from * to end of round; sl st to first sc of round to join. (32 [35, 38, 44, 47, 50, 50] sc)

Fasten off.

Weave in remaining ends.

Girls Sweater

Skill Level: Easy +

Supplies:

US Size J, 6.0 mm crochet hook

Easy Crochet Sweaters & Shawls

Measuring Tape

Tapestry Needle

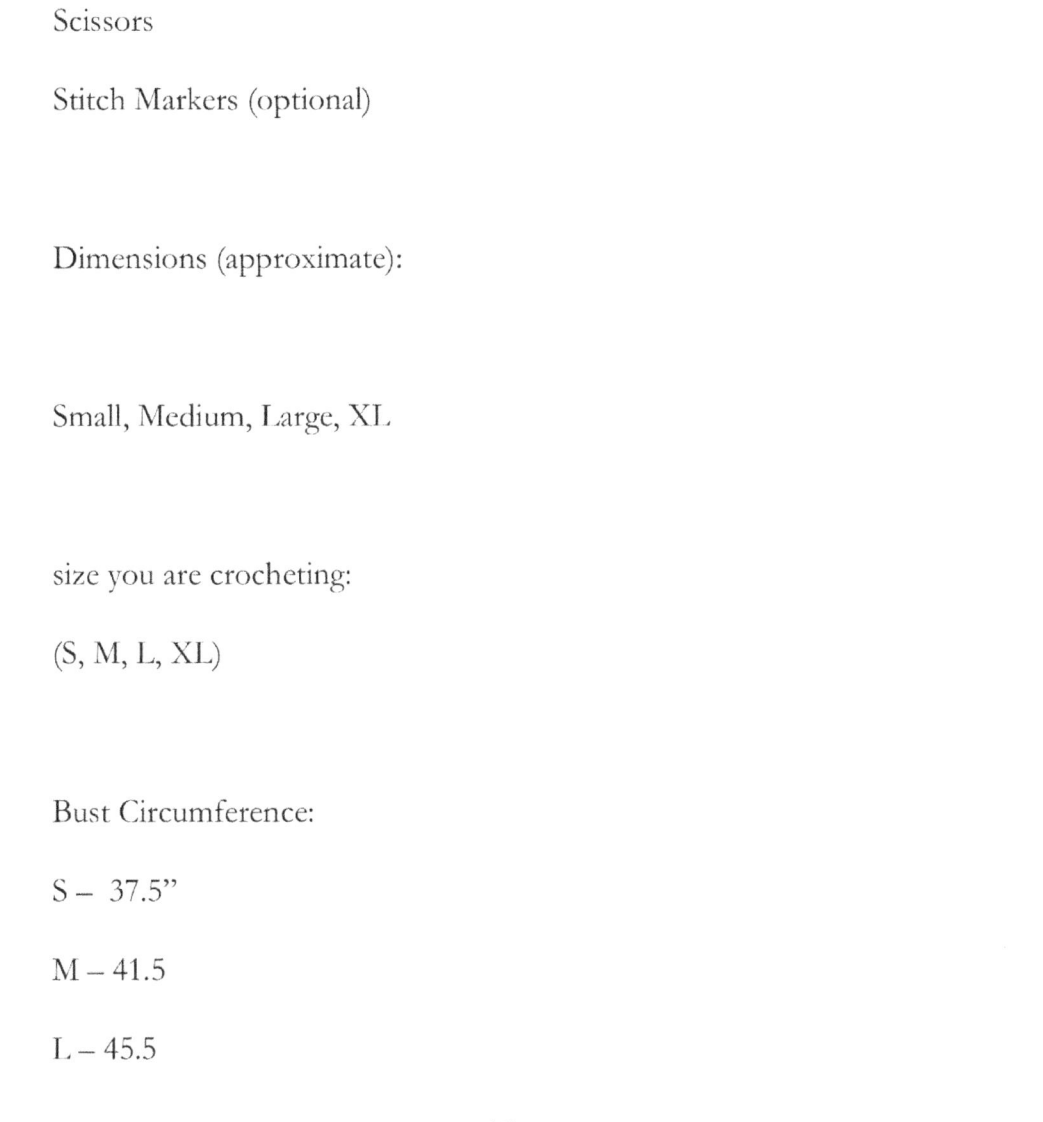

Scissors

Stitch Markers (optional)

Dimensions (approximate):

Small, Medium, Large, XL

size you are crocheting:

(S, M, L, XL)

Bust Circumference:

S – 37.5"

M – 41.5

L – 45.5

XL – 49.5

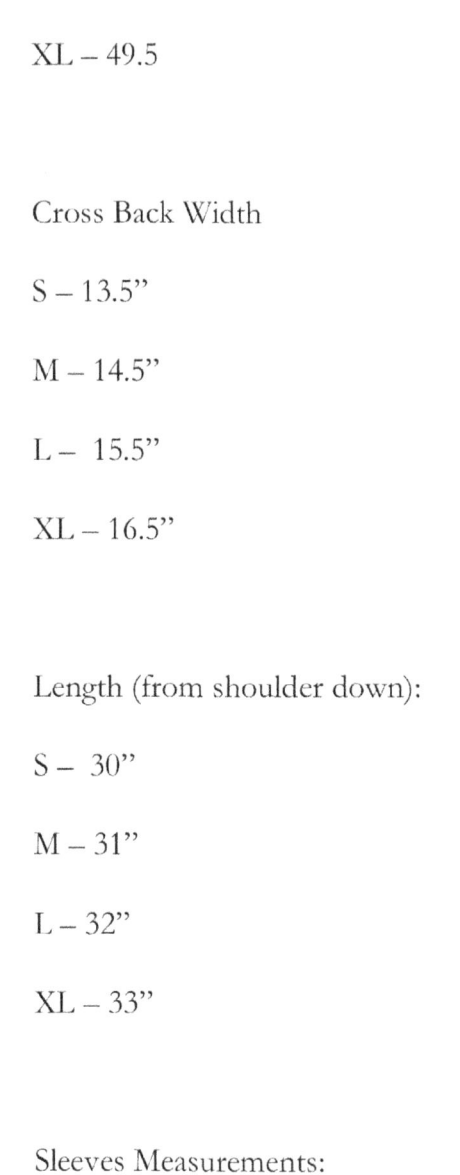

Cross Back Width

S – 13.5"

M – 14.5"

L – 15.5"

XL – 16.5"

Length (from shoulder down):

S – 30"

M – 31"

L – 32"

XL – 33"

Sleeves Measurements:

Easy Crochet Sweaters & Shawls

Length: (19", 19", 19.5", 19.5")

Approximate circumference at widest point of upper portion of sleeve: (13", 15", 17", 19")

Approximate circumference at sleeve cuff: (8", 10", 12", 14")

Abbreviations & Skills:

ch – chain

dc – double crochet

hdc – half double crochet

hdc flo – half double crochet through the front loop only

yo – yarn over

FPdc – front post double crochet

BPdc – back post double crochet

Easy Crochet Sweaters & Shawls

Special Stitch

Bean Stitch – bean st – Row 1 Ch 2, turn, insert hook in 3rd st from hook, pull up a loop, yo, insert hook in same st, pull up another loop (4 loops on hook) yo, insert hook in same st (6 loops on hook) yo, pull through all 6 loops on hook (bean st made), *ch1, sk st, work bean st in next st; repeat from * across the row.

Gauge:

Approximately 11 ¾ stitches and approximately 7 rows in 4" x 4" of double crochet

Notes:

This cardigan is made up of three rectangular panels which are seamed together at the sides. The sleeves are then crocheted by attaching the yarn to the arm openings and crocheting in rounds. Adjustments to the width of the cardigan can be made by crocheting each panel for more rows.

Easy Crochet Sweaters & Shawls

Pattern Instructions

Rectangular Front Panel of Cardigan (make 2)

Ch (117, 121, 123, 125)

Row 1 Hdc in 3rd st from hook and in each ch st across the row (115, 119, 121, 123)

Row 2 Ch 2 (doesn't count as st), turn, hdc flo in 3rd st from hook and in each st across the row (115, 119, 121, 123)

Row 3 Repeat row 2

Row 4 Work the bean st pattern across the row (refer to Special Stitch section)

Rows 5 – 7 Repeat row 2 (115, 119, 121, 123) (note: in row 5 you will work in each ch st and st across the row)

Row 8 Work the bean st pattern across the row

Row 9 Repeat row 2

Row 10 Work the bean st pattern across the row

Crossed Double Crochet Section

Rows 11 – 14 Ch 3 (counts as dc here and throughout pattern), turn, dc in next st, *sk st, dc in next st, dc in skipped st; repeat from * across to last st, dc in last st of row. (115, 119, 121, 123)

(note: last st of row in rows 12-14 will be the turn ch of previous row)

Double Crochet Section

Row 15 Ch 3, turn, dc in each st across the row (115, 119, 121, 123)

Rows 16 – (23, 26, 29, 32) or until panel measures approximately (12", 13.5", 15", 16.5") across, repeat row 15

Tie off and weave in ends.

Rectangular Back Panel

Ch (117, 121, 123, 125)

Row 1 Dc in 4th ch from hook and in each ch st across the row (115, 119, 121, 123)

Row 2 Ch 3 (counts as st here and throughout pattern), turn, dc in next dc st and in each st across the row (115, 119, 121, 123)

Repeat row 2 for approximately (24, 25, 27, 29) rows or until piece measures approximately (13.5", 14.5", 15.5", 16.5")

Tie off and weave in ends.

Assembly

Next, place each side panel along the long sides of the back panel. The Double Crochet Sections of the front panels should be lined up with each long edge of the back panel. With a length of yarn and a tapestry needle, seam approximately (22", 23", 24", 25") up each side. Tie off and weave in ends.

Next, leave a space for the arm opening measuring (6.5", 7.5", 8.5", 9.5") long. Attach yarn at top of arm opening and seam up the remainder of the panels. Tie off and weave in ends. (see picture)

Easy Crochet Sweaters & Shawls

Sleeves (do not turn at end of each round)

Attach yarn to bottom of arm opening

Place stitch marker at beginning of each round

Row 1 Work (38, 44, 49, 55) double crochet stitches evenly around, sl st to join in top of beg ch 3 (don't turn here or throughout sleeve pattern)

Row 2 Ch 3 (counts as dc), dc in each st around, sl st to join in top of beg ch 3 (38, 44, 49, 55)

Row 3 Ch 3, dc in each st around to last 2 sts, dc2tog (decrease), sl st to join in top of beg ch 3

Row 4 Ch 3 (counts as dc), dc in each st around, sl st to join in top of beg ch 3

Row 5 Ch 3 (counts as dc), dc in each st around, sl st to join in top of beg ch 3

Repeat rows 3 – 5 until sleeve measures approximately (17.5", 17.5", 18", 18"). The stitch count will decrease by one stitch every third row.

Next, you'll crochet the cuff of the sleeve.

Sleeve Cuff

Ch 3, work FPhdc, followed by BPhdc. Repeat this pattern, alternating a FPhdc st, followed by a BPhdc st around.

Continue working this pattern in rounds, working FPdc stitches in each FPdc st, and BPdc stitches in each BPdc stitch around for a total of about 1.5" – 2" or until you've reached your desired length. Tie off and weave in ends. (To make the ribbing work out perfectly, work an even number of stiches around)

Repeat this sleeve pattern for each arm opening.

Finishing

Block to shape and size as necessary.

Optional:

Add a button or two in order to be able to close the front of the sweater. You may also consider adding a belt to secure the sweater when worn.

Easy Crochet Sweaters & Shawls

Tapestry Crochet Fisherman's Sweater

Supplies:

- Lion Brand LB Collection Merino Yak Alpaca (Weight: 4/medium – 126 yds, 1.75oz)

Easy Crochet Sweaters & Shawls

– Navy (#498-110) – 7 (7/8/9/9/11/12/13) balls

- Lion Brand Fishermen's Wool (Weight: 4/Medium – 465yds, 8oz)

– Natural (#150-098) – 1 ball

- Size H (5.0 mm) crochet hook

- Tapestry needle

- Stitch markers

Sizes/Measurements:

- XS: Length: 19", Bust: 34", Upper arm: 12"

- S: Length: 20", Bust: 36", Upper arm: 13"

- M: Length: 21", Bust: 38", Upper arm: 14"

- L: Length: 22", Bust, 42", Upper arm: 15"

- XL: Length: 22", Bust: 46", Upper arm: 16"

- 2XL: Length: 23", Bust: 50", Upper arm: 17"

- 3XL: Length: 24", Bust: 54", Upper arm: 18"

- 4XL: Length: 25", Bust: 58", Upper arm: 19"

Easy Crochet Sweaters & Shawls

Gauge:

• 4" = 14.5 stitches (measure on a dc row) 4" = 10.5 rows

• NB: you should have 5.5 rows of dc and 5 rows of sc with the color work to make 4" = 10.5 rows

Abbreviations and Glossary (US Terms):

Ch – chain

Sc – single crochet

Dc – double crochet

Rs – right side

Ws – wrong side

Fpdc – front post double crochet

Bpdc – back post double crochet

Overall Pattern Notes:

- The Seafarer is designed as a shorter length sweater; remember to check the gauge and your measurements before you begin.

Front Of Sweater

The color work will always be done right side facing. You will need to keep your tension fairly loose to make the color work effective, refer to the videos for help with this.

Divide 1 skein of Fisherman wool into 3 equally sized balls (approx. 75g each)

Loosely ch 61 (64, 70, 79, 88, 94, 100, 109)

Row 1: First dc into 3rd chain from hook and then dc into every ch st. This will give you a total of:

59 (62, 68, 77, 86, 92, 98, 107) dc for this row, ch 1, turn.

It is a good idea to check at this point that your work measures approximately:

XS: 17-18" /S: 18-19"/M: 19-20"/L: 21-22"/XL: 23-24"/2XL: 25-26"/3XL: 27-28"/4XL: 29-30"

Row 2: Begin color work. Take the ends of each of the 3 balls of Fishermen's wool you have made and hold together to make one strand. Holding this at the back of your work, insert hook into the first stitch and make 1sc over the 3 strands of Fishermen's wool. It is important to hold the yarn you are carrying at the back of your work and to keep your work reasonably loose.

Repeat x1

Now, for the 3rd stitch of this row you will make an arrow/heart shaped sc stitch using the 3 strands of Fishermen's wool and the tapestry crochet technique. So, insert your hook into the stitch, pull the 3 strands through, yarn over in navy and pull through all 4 strands of wool on your hook (3x Natural , 1 x Navy)

You will repeat this pattern of sc2 in navy followed by 1 arrow/heart sc in natural until the end of the row, you should finish the row with sc2 in navy, ch 1, turn.

Row 3: Dc 59 (62, 68, 77, 86, 92, 98, 107) in navy, ch1, turn.

Row 4: Repeat color work Row 2. Sc2 in navy (carrying natural), 1 arrow sc st in natural (carrying navy) and repeat until the end of the row.

Cut your fishermen's wool, leaving enough to sew in the ends, do not cut the navy/main color yarn!

Repeat Rows 1 and 2 for the number of rows indicated:

XS x16/S x17/M x18/L x19/XLx19/2XLx20/3XLx21/4XLx22

Total number of rows before beginning neckline, (including 1 +2):

XS: 34

S: 36

M: 38

L: 40

XL: 40

2XL: 42

3XL: 44

4XL: 46

Row (39): Dc 59 (62, 68, 77, 86, 92, 98, 107) ch1, turn.

Begin Neckline:

Left neckline:

Easy Crochet Sweaters & Shawls

Row 1: Color work row, sc 21 (23, 26, 30, 35, 38, 41, 45) ch1, turn

Row 2: 1 dc decrease, dc 19 (21, 24, 28, 33, 36, 39, 43) ch1, turn

Row 3: Color work row, sc 20 (22, 25, 29, 34, 37, 40, 44) ch1, turn

Row 4: 1 dc decrease, dc 18 (20, 23, 27, 32, 35, 38, 42) ch1, turn

Row 5: Color work row, sc19 (21, 24, 28, 33, 36, 39, 43) ch1, turn

Row 6: 1 dc decrease, dc 17 (19, 22, 26, 31, 34, 37, 41) ch1, turn

Row 7: Color work row, sc 18 (20, 23, 27, 32, 35, 38, 42) ch1, turn

Row 8: 1 dc decrease, dc 16 (18, 21, 25, 30, 33, 36, 40) ch1, turn

Row 9: Color work row, sc 17 (19, 22, 26, 31, 34, 37, 41) ch1, turn

Row 10: dc 17 (19, 22, 26, 31, 34, 37, 41) ch1, turn

Row 11: Color work row, sc 17 (19, 22, 26, 31, 34, 37, 41) ch1, turn

Row 12: dc 17 (19, 22, 26, 31, 34, 37, 41) ch1, turn

Right neckline:

Row 1: Color work row, so start rs facing. Counting in from the edge of your work (arm hole side), join yarn to the 21st (23rd, 26th, 30th, 35th, 38th, 41st, 45th) st in, this should leave you with 16 sts in the middle for the neck for sizes s/m/xl/2xl/3xl and 17 sts for xs/l/4xl. Begin a color work row as usual with 2sc in navy followed by 1 in natural, sc 21 (23, 26, 30, 35, 38, 41, 45) in total, ch 1, turn

Easy Crochet Sweaters & Shawls

Row 2: dc 19 (21, 24, 28, 33, 36, 39, 43), 1dc decrease, ch1, turn

Row 3: Color work row, this time you will need to start with 1sc in navy followed by 1sc in natural before continuing the usual 2sc navy and 1sc natural pattern. Sc 20 (22, 25, 29, 34, 37, 40, 44) in total, ch1, turn

Row 4: dc 18 (20, 23, 27, 32, 35, 38, 42), 1dc decrease, ch1, turn

Row 5: Color work row, 1 sc in natural, 2sc in navy, and continue the usual pattern, sc19 (21, 24, 28, 33, 36, 39, 43) in total, ch1, turn

Row 6: dc 17 (19, 22, 26, 31, 34, 37, 41) 1 dc decrease, ch1, turn

Row 7: Color work row, 2 sc in navy to start, sc 18 (20, 23, 27, 32, 35, 38, 42) in total ch1, turn

Row 8: dc 16 (18, 21, 25, 30, 33, 36, 40) 1 dc decrease, ch1, turn

Row 9: Color work row,1 sc in navy to start, sc 17 (19, 22, 26, 31, 34, 37, 41) in total ch1, turn

Row 10: dc 17 (19, 22, 26, 31, 34, 37, 41) ch1, turn

Row 11: Color work row, 1 sc in navy to start sc 17 (19, 22, 26, 31, 34, 37, 41) in total ch1, turn

Row 12: dc 17 (19, 22, 26, 31, 34, 37, 41) ch1, turn

You can of course, sew in all those ends of Fishermen's wool at this point, but if you are feeling brave you could try a crochet hack if sewing in ends is not your thing. If you sew along the edge with your sewing machine, you can cut the ends very short and do exactly zero sewing in here.

Easy Crochet Sweaters & Shawls

Back Of Sweater:

Gauge swatch 4" x 4" = Back of sweater

4" = 14.5 st

4" = 8 rows

Loosely ch 61 (64, 70, 79, 88, 94, 100, 109)

Row 1: First dc into 3rd chain from hook and then dc into every ch st. This will give you a total of:

59 (62, 68, 77, 86, 92, 98, 107) dc for this row, ch 1, turn.

Repeat Row 1 35(37/39/41/43/45/47/49) more times (36/38/40/42/44/46/48/50 rows total)

Begin construction

Right sides facing sc the shoulder seams together.

Now, looking at the front of your garment, WS facing, sc the sides together leaving a gap of 15 (17, 18, 19, 21, 22, 23,25) rows for the armhole. Count the rows on the front of your sweater.

Sleeves

Turn the body right side out again and attach yarn to center of underarm sleeve opening (you should make your first dc into this space.)

Round 1: (RS) You need to evenly space 46 (48/52/56/60/64/68/72) dc stitches around the armhole. Sl st to join.

Note: To avoid holes when joining your arm, you can actually pick up part of the previous stitch on the dc rows of the front and back of your sweater. See photos below.

Round 2: dc into each dc all the way round. Sl st to join.

Repeat Round 2, 7 more times for all sizes.

Round 3: dc2tog and dc into each dc all the way round. Sl st to join.

Repeat Round 3 for approximately 25 more rounds or until the sleeve reaches the wrist.

Neck ribbing:

Easy Crochet Sweaters & Shawls

Round 1: (RS facing) Working in Fishermen's wool, start at the back and work dc25 along the back neckline. Next, evenly space dc along the front. You should have approx. 78 dc stitches when you reach the end of the first round, join.

Round 2 + 3: frpdc, bpdc until the end of the round, sl st to join.

Bottom of the sweater ribbing:

Round 1: (RS facing) dc all the way around, join. You should have approx. 117 (123, 135, 153, 171, 183, 195, 213) dc stitches.

Round 2 + 3: frpdc, bpdc all the way around, join.

Sleeve Ribbing:

Round 1: (RS facing) dc all the way around, join. The final stitch count for each size will vary depending on how long you have made your sleeves.

Round 2 + 3: frpdc, bpdc all the way around, join.

Sew in the ends and enjoy your beautiful sweater!

Lace Crochet Shawl

Supplies:

Green Elephant Yarn Fingering Weight /425m/4 ply Sock: 75% SW Merino Wool/25% Nylon/100gr) in colourway Under the Sea

A small amount of a contrast yarn for tassels

Easy Crochet Sweaters & Shawls

4.5mm crochet hook, or whatever hook size gives a loose tension

You can use 425m of any fingering weight yarn or yarn weight of your choice and matching hook.

Measurements

Shawl measures 66 in [168cm] wide x 25 in [63.5cm] depth

Notes

The main body is worked in one piece from bottom-up, increasing on each side until a triangle is made.

The shawl can be made larger or smaller by working more or fewer pattern repeats. This will alter the amount of yarn required.

You can use any Fingering weight yarn to achieve a similar effect

Includes written instructions. Pattern written in US crochet terms

Gauge is not important.

Abbreviations

US Crochet Terms

Beg — beginning

Ch — chain

St — stitch

Sc — single crochet

Dc — double crochet

Tr — treble crochet

Sp — space

UK Crochet Terms

Beg — beginning

Ch — chain

St — stitch

Dc — double crochet

Tr — treble crochet

Dtr — double treble crochet

Easy Crochet Sweaters & Shawls

Sp   space

Special Stitches

2 Double Crochet Cluster (2 dc cl): Yo, insert hook in space indicated, yo, pull up a loop, yo, pull through 2 loops, yo, insert hook in same space, yo, pull up a loop, yo, pull through 2 loops, yo, pull through 3 loops on hook.

V-Stitch (V-st): [1 dc, ch 1, 1 dc] in stitch indicated in pattern

Shell: [2 dc cl, ch 2, 2 dc cl, ch 2, 2 dc cl] in space/st indicated in pattern

Instructions for Crochet One Skein Lace Shawl

Using 4.5mm hook make a magic ring

Row 1: Ch 6 (counts as 1 tr, ch 2 here and throughout), v-st (see special stitches), ch 2, 1 tr in magic ring, turn and pull ring tight – 2 tr, 1 x v-st, 2 x ch-2

Easy Crochet Sweaters & Shawls

Row 2: Ch 1 (does not count as a st here and throughout), 1 sc in 1st st, ch 1, shell (see special stitches) in next v-st, ch 1, 1 sc in 4th st of beg ch 6, turn – 1 shell, 2 sc, 2 x ch-1

Row 3: Ch 6, v-st in 1st st (the sc at base of ch 6), ch 2, 1 sc in centre of next shell (insert hook in top of centre 2 dc cl), ch 2, [v-st, ch 2, 1 tr] in last st, turn – 2 tr, 2 x v-st, 1 sc, 4 x ch-2

Row 4: Ch 1, 1 sc in 1st st, ch 1, shell in next v-st, ch 1, 1 sc in next sc, ch 1, shell in next v-st, ch 1, 1 sc in 4th ch of beg ch 6, turn – 2 shell, 3 sc, 4 x ch-1

Row 5: Ch 6, v-st in 1st st, ch 2, sc in centre of next shell, ch 2, v-st in next sc, ch 2, sc in centre of next shell, ch 2, [v-st, ch 2, 1 tr] in last st, turn – 2 tr, 3 x v-st, 2 sc, 6 x ch-2

Row 6: Ch 1, 1 sc in 1st st, * ch 1, shell in next v-st, ch 1, 1 sc in next sc; rep from * across making last sc in 4th ch of beg ch 6, turn

Row 7: Ch 6, v-st in 1st st, * ch 2, sc in centre of next shell, ch 2, v-st in next sc; rep from * across ending last repeat with [v-st, ch 2, 1 tr] in last st, turn

Rows 6 & 7 form pattern repeat

Rows 8 – 54: repeat rows 6 & 7. Fasten off yarn.

Finishing

Weave in all loose ends. Soak your shawl in lukewarm water and gently wring in a towel. Lay project out to finished size and pull gently into shape. Pin in place and leave to dry. Take your time pinning your shawl…….it will make a huge difference to the finished piece! Add tassels if you wish.

Tassel Instructions

Make 3 tassels as follows:

Using a book approx. 6-8" in width, cut a 12" length of yarn and lay across top of book – this will be used to tie top of tassel. Wrap yarn around book about 30 times (depending on thickness required). Using the 12" tie, knot top of tassel tightly. Cut tassel at opposite end. Wrap another length of yarn around tassel 1" from top approx..5 times and knot ends together. Trim if needed and sew securely to 3 corners of shawl.

Easy Crochet Sweaters & Shawls

Summer Nights Crochet Shawl

Supplies:

Summer Nights Yarn from Lion Brand Yarn less than 874 yards (2 skeins) or any Super Fine 1 weight yarn

4.5 mm crochet hook

yarn needle

scissors

Crochet Abbreviations

sc = single crochet

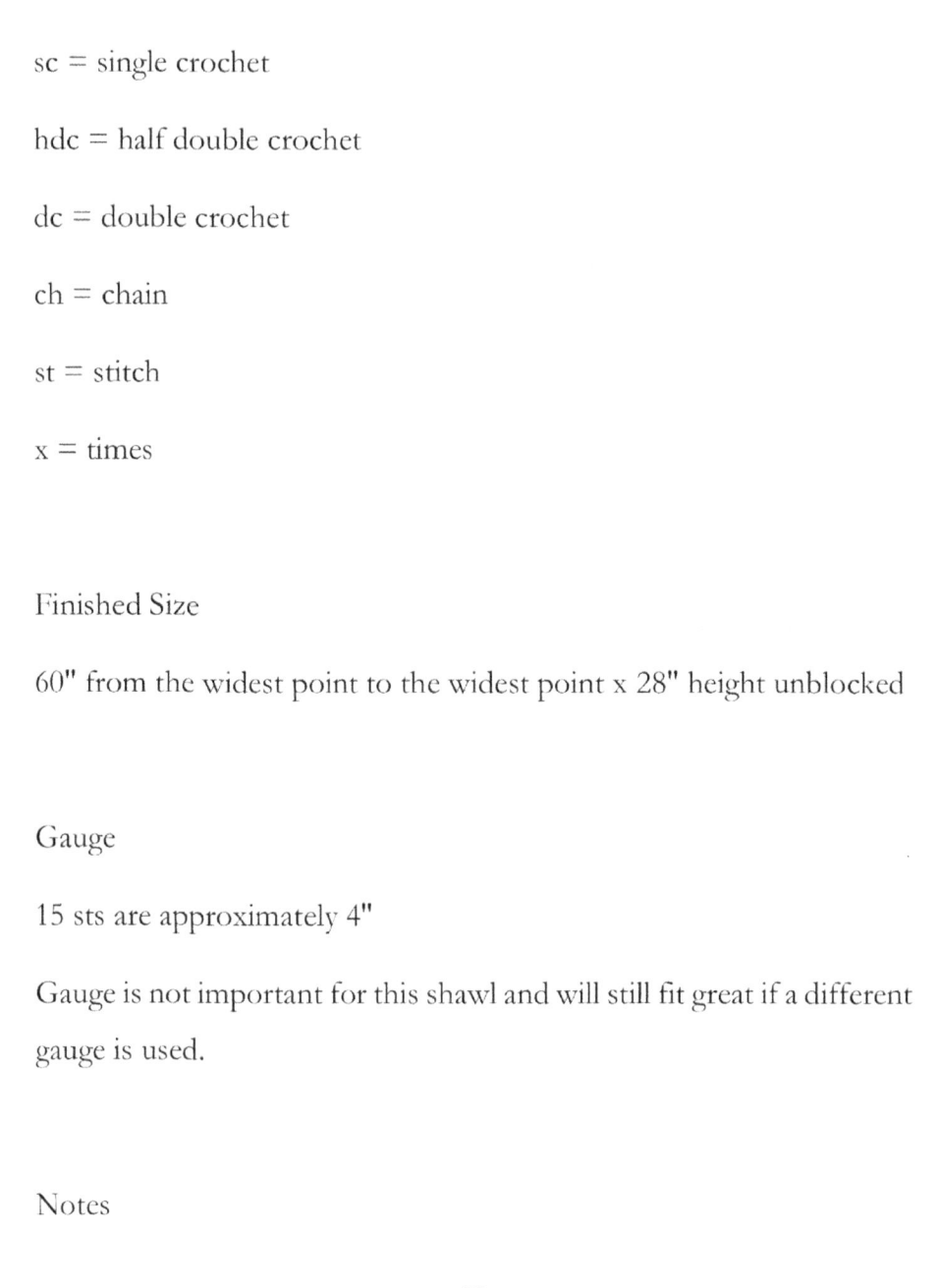

hdc = half double crochet

dc = double crochet

ch = chain

st = stitch

x = times

Finished Size

60" from the widest point to the widest point x 28" height unblocked

Gauge

15 sts are approximately 4"

Gauge is not important for this shawl and will still fit great if a different gauge is used.

Notes

Easy Crochet Sweaters & Shawls

Please read note section to fully understand the pattern

The entire pattern is worked holding 2 skeins of yarn together at the same time.

ch 1's do NOT count as a ST

ch 3's at the beginning of the row DO count as a dc st.

Each row will start with a ch 3, dc 2x in the next st

Each row will end with a 3 dc's in the top of the turning chain from the row before.

Written in standard US terms

The Easy Crochet Shawl Pattern

*see the stitch chart below the pattern for extra help with stitch placement for the first 4 rows.

Row 1: Start with a ch 3, in the 3rd ch from the hook dc 2 times, ch 2, dc 3 times in the same stitch, turn. (6)

Row 2: ch 3, 2 dc in first st, sk 2 st's and ch 1, dc 3 times in the ch 2 space from the row before, ch 2, dc 3 more times in the same ch 2 space, sk 2 sts, ch 1, end with 3 dc's in the last st, turn. (12)

Row 3: ch 3, dc 2 times in the first st, ch 1, dc, hdc, sc in the next ch 1 space, ch 1, dc 3 times in the next ch 2 space from the row before, ch 2, dc 3 times in the same ch 2 space, ch 1, sc, hdc, dc in the next ch 1 space, ch 1, sk 2 sts, dc 3 times into the last st(or turning ch), turn. (18)

Row 4: ch 3, dc 2 times in the first st, ch 1, * dc, hdc, sc, in the next ch 1 space, ch 1, repeat from * 1 time, dc 3 times in the next ch 2 space from the row before, ch 2, dc 3 times in the same space, ch 1, **sc, hdc, d, ch 1 in the next ch 1 space from the row before, repeat from * 1 time, dc 3 times in the top of the last st (or turning ch), turn. (24)

Row 5 – 28: The remaining rows are worked like row 4 but since we are increasing each round there will always be two more chain 1 spaces in each row to work into. For example, in row 3 there were 4 chain 1 spaces, in row 4 there were 6 chain 1 spaces which means that each row has an increase of six stitches since we always work 3 stitches into each ch 1 space.

Row 29 – 35: Work the same as row 4 but use ONLY double crochets in place of the single and half double crochets throughout the remaining rows.

Since there are TWO additional chain 1 spaces in each round then we will always have an increase of SIX stitches in each round.

The count of each round will be as follows starting with row 5

Stitch Count for Rows 5- 35: 30,36,42,48,54,60,66,72,78,84,90,96,102,108,114,120,126,132,138,144, 150,156, 162,168,174,180,186,192,198, 204 & 210

Easy Crochet Sweaters & Shawls

Finishing: Fasten off and weave in loose ends with a yarn needle

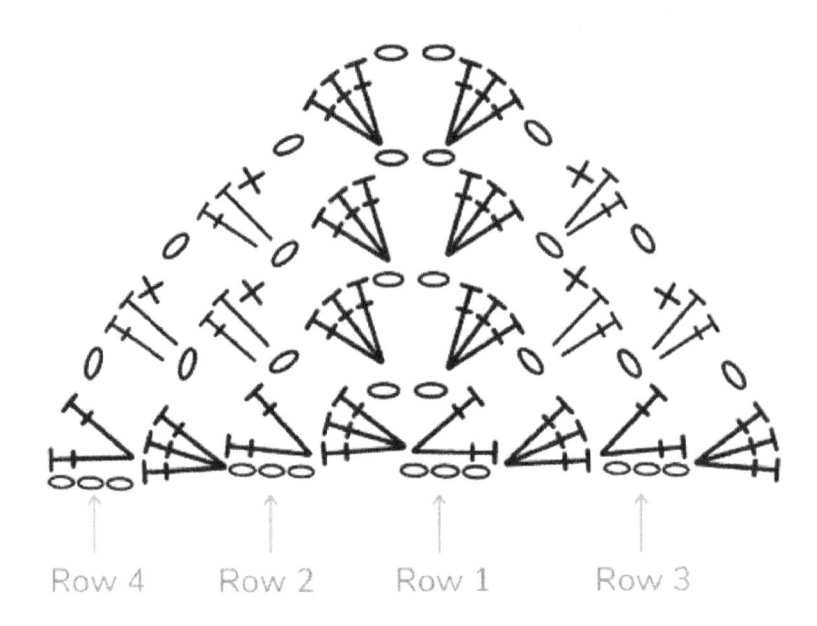

Row 4   Row 2   Row 1   Row 3

Made in the USA
Coppell, TX
01 May 2025